Healing your inner child:

overcoming trauma & ptsd,Emotional and
psychological becoming the best version of
yourself by forgiving yourself.

By

Prof.Henry A.Harrison

Table of contents

Introduction

What is your inner child?

What Is An Inner Child & What Does It Know?
what-is-an-inner-child

What is an inner kid and what does it know?
Our inner child is a part of ourselves that's been there ever since we were created, through utero, and all the developmental years following when we were young and maturing into delicate selves: baby, infant, toddler, young kid, and middle school year.

The inner child may frequently remember happy memories as well as early anxieties, traumas, neglect, or profound loss. It might be hard to identify the particular incident that is pulling at us, but we can start to discover the internal patterns that have left us subconscious "bread crumb trails" as we start to explore our inner world.

Each one of us has an "inner child" residing within.

You have an inner kid. I have an inner kid. We all do. Your "inner child" is a portion of your subconscious that has been collecting signals far before it was ready to properly absorb what was going on (mentally and emotionally) (mentally and emotionally). It stores emotions, memories, and beliefs from the past as well as aspirations and goals for the future.

Our customers are often interested and delighted when we discuss inner child work and how we all have a little one (or small ones) inside of us. When we provide room for inner child healing, we typically observe a change in clients' healing and general development towards clarity of the self and better therapy success.

How can we recognize our Inner Child parts?
Our inner kid is the one who recalls the lovely fragrance of grandma as she reached down to embrace us, with a tremendous expression of joy on her face when we showed her how we were able to ride our bike.

Our inner child recalls the sensation of our hearts filling with excitement and love when our dad looked at us with a sparkle in his eyes when we shared our favorite toy with the neighbor.

Our inner kid recalls getting invited to a friend's birthday celebration and feeling so delighted and confident.

Our inner child is also the one who felt the salty tears stream down our cheeks as mother left the home in a panic to go say goodbye to her dad while he was dying.

Our inner child recalls being neglected and tormented on the bus on the first day of school.

Our inner kid recalls feeling foolish when the instructor mocked us or when we didn't have the solution to a "seemingly easy" inquiry.

Our inner kid is there when we start our first work, convincing our supervisor that we're responsible and competent, feeling proud.

Our inner kid is there when we are teens, desiring so strongly to belong.
Our inner child is within us as we start on a search to discover love, or to find social groups to join.
It's the portion that feels accepted, peaceful, pleasant, and cozy when we have nice moments with people.

It's also the portion that feels crushed and betrayed when we are mistreated, neglected, or lied to when someone hurts or betrays us.

Our inner child is continually speaking with us...
we only need to learn to listen.
Now, our inner child may either be quiet and comfortable (for the most part), or it can act out and make things a little rumbly within, standing in the way of good relationships, organizing skills, and self-control.

Our inner kid may either make it or break it when it comes to becoming a useful member of society...or steps toward finding pleasure.

If you're feeling irritated or trapped in any element of your life, it's probably that your inner child is requiring some care. Stuck spots might appear like a difficulty at job work, in parenting, finding or retaining love, expanding relationships, or creating boundaries.

When the inner child dominates the show
You may discover that you're feeling dread, perfectionism, or anxiety or are avoiding specific individuals, locations or activities. These are all ways that your inner kid is seeking to feel protected. When the inner child is running the show, it'll make actions, choices, and ideas based on unconscious beliefs or experiences from the past and depending on what the inner self would require to feel secure.

Often, the inner child does not have access to the adult "self" reality and may not know about how life is different today, or how things have changed.

Childhood emotional scars might make you feel like you're going around with a ton of bricks on your back.

If your inner child is going around with 50 pounds of anguish, you may feel like you are carrying the weight of the world on your shoulders. If your inner child lived with instability, uncertainty, or danger, it may hold you back from making changes. You may notice a scared side, apprehensive of you attempting new things, yet, if you are willing to go on with your life you'll probably feel conflicted.

Why we become stuck: when one half craves safety and predictability while another part desires potential, connection, and adventure.
You can find a medium ground, and "unstuck" so that you can go through obstructions. To nurture the balance of creativity, flexibility, responsibility, connectedness, and consistency, it'll be vital for your adult self and kid self to meet and get to know each other. This is the first step to forming a collaborative team- one

where your adult need and inner child wants are addressed.

Two Steps To Cultivating a Relationship with your Inner Child
Two steps are necessary here:

ONE: Getting in touch with your inner child, having a discussion, and forming a connection with it.

TWO: Beginning to truly tune in, and learn about your inner child's needs, sufferings, hopes, and dreams.....and taking measures to make them materialize.

Our meditation on Connecting with your Inner Child is meant to encourage you in coming in touch with your inner child. Our objective is for you to tap into how your inner child is doing, provide it with some compassionate care, and find a method to address its needs. Often, doing this helps offer clarity on what has to alter for you to go ahead. As also, this internal process can ease the reluctance and "stuckness" you are experiencing in your adult life.

For some, "reparenting" the inner child is useful as well, in this process.)

Accessing the inner child to lighten the stresses and encourage hope and pleasure.
Begin here....
To achieve this, we begin by asking your adult self to be a bit open and potentially, vulnerable. For your inner child to come out of hiding and to speak about what is going on or what it's wanting, we need to be open to hearing and seeing its tale; inquiring about its life, aspirations, dreams, anxieties, and worries.

We want your inner child to begin forming a trusting connection with your adult self so it may share honestly. We want to know about its aspirations, dreams, desires, its words,.... as well as its grief, its anguish, its concerns, and its worries.

Often, we observe that when the inner child has someone (adult you) who loves and slows down, and is there with it, it can calm down and experience the sensations that it had to brush aside for years. It's generally suggested to perform this work with a professional therapist who deals with inner child work, childhood emotional neglect, or emotional aches since the work may be painful and a qualified clinician can assist guide you and encourage the healing.

As you learn to know your inner child you may realize that it needs some crucial healing.
There are many different methods to provide support, love, and healing to the inner child. It may need to tell you a narrative that it's kept a secret for years. It may need to show you the loss and pain it suffered years ago but never got to grieve. It may want to show you its need for affection and attention and for you to discover methods to have those needs satisfied in life before you go on with the 'work project' you've been working on.

It may call for you to speak out in your relationships since it doesn't want to be ignored as you used to be, as a youngster. Or it may be something else. We don't know what will come up until we start this procedure.

Once the inner child knows it has your attention and you are trying your best to provide it love and fulfill its needs it'll frequently be more receptive to you.

It may require greater physical or emotional safety, more attention to the way you're taking care (of your mind, body, or soul), healing previous wounds, creating boundaries in life, or adjusting who you spend time with. This effort will typically expose whatever is genuinely essential.

We've observed how many symptoms alter and clients begin moving past and through stuck areas when we engage with the deeper levels of inner child healing. We've witnessed customers begin opening their hearts to expanding the love in their lives, or for the first time, actually letting love in. For others, completing the deeper work helps them to finally be present in their parenting as they can connect without the irritation that used to be there. For others, they start coming up to work, and relationships with confidence, and more easily ask for what they need. For others, the worry and dread they were harboring reduce dramatically and they can stand by the limits they've been attempting to establish for years.

Successful individuals have a satisfied inner child

By success, I don't mean those who are famous or affluent, but people who have love, feel comfortable being in their skin, have a feeling of inner peace, and feel satisfied. A healthy inner child is rich in love, relationships, psychologically, feeling satisfied in their sense of significance, and able to withstand the aches of ups and downs of life. Successful individuals aren't merely those who are brilliant and "made it". My notion of success relates to emotionally controlled individuals, who have a healthy connection with their emotions and have a quiet inner child.

What does a joyful inner kid look and feel like?

When our inner kid (and our "internal family") is peaceful, we have the green light to go ahead and attempt new things. We know we can handle failure or slip-ups. We can cope with tiny levels of guilt without becoming eaten up by terror. We know we are solid and don't need to behave hastily. We don't become caught in our effort to obtain acceptance from others.

If our inner kid feels comfortable and solid, it will enable us to flourish.
It's like an anchor. If the inner child feels shaky, as adults, we will feel uncertain, bewildered, and disorganized in life. When our inner child feels firm, its anchor is well planted and we feel, and come across, more clear, confident, and secure.

Now, how can you know whether your inner kid has any pains
Feelings of humiliation, remorse, and/or anguish.

Chronic overworking and needing to accomplish (to obtain acceptance or belonging) (to get approval or belonging).

Inability to be present at the moment.

Regular worry and terror.

Rigid and attempting to be "perfect" (cannot take failure) (cannot handle a failure).

Difficulty seeing and enjoying "wins" in life (no win can ever be enough) (no win will ever be enough).

Unhealthy relationship practices and/or avoiding relationships and affection.
Self-sabotage and obsessive/addictive behavior.
Underachieving.
Rumination and negative self-talk.

Ways to help with repairing your inner child
Utilize activities to start feeling (a little bit at a time) to reverse the numbness.

Work on lowering worries and fears by analyzing scary memories or events.

Developing healthy connections that enable you to feel comfortable and solid in the world.

Creating a warm and welcoming atmosphere.

Create structure and nutritious self-care- by developing stable rhythms of food, sleeping, hygiene & sex.

Develop distinct emotional, energy, temporal, and physical limits.

Create interests and hobbies and make them part of your life.

Shift attention from performance to doing + being + celebrating.

Shift your inner ideas (what beliefs you feed yourself, counseling might assist with this) (what beliefs you feed yourself, therapy can help with this).

Ready to take a step to connect with or improve your connection with your inner child?

Chapter 1

Connecting and Reconnecting with your inner child.

As you develop, you naturally get alienated from your inner child. The demands of adult life–money, relationships, work–overshadow the connection. Though you may not feel connected to your inner kid, it's always there, affecting your feelings and actions from the background.

Whether or not you had an unhappy or terrible upbringing, your inner child clings to both good and bad feelings. When you reconnect with it, you confront those feelings as an adult and begin to recover from your prior experiences.

SIGNS OF A WOUNDED INNER CHILD

Everyone has concerns and worries from childhood, but not everyone has a wounded inner child. Some symptoms you could have as a wounded inner child are...

You feel the want to disguise your feelings, such as holding back tears or pretending like you aren't upset even though you are.

You believe your value is related to your production or achievement. If you aren't the greatest, you're the worst.

You avoid confrontation at all costs, instead fleeing difficult circumstances or following the route of least resistance.

You're a people pleaser and like to rush to others for assistance on significant personal choices.

You have problems creating and sustaining appropriate boundaries, particularly with your parents or in romantic relationships.

You respond violently to even light criticism, either by closing down, breaking down, or exploding out.

All that being said, everyone can benefit from inner child work. We all retain scars from our childhoods, but some are worse than others.

BENEFITS OF INNER CHILD WORK

When we speak about "inner child work," we mean reconnecting with that subconscious part of yourself to enjoy the youthful pleasures of life and address the conditioning we got as children. By undertaking the work as an adult, you may start to recover from prior events and deconstruct your ideas about the world and yourself.

For example, assume you grew up being instructed to eat all the food on your plate at every meal. As an adult, you can still feel bad about not completing meals or have a problematic relationship with eating in general. When you reconnect with your inner child, you start to understand where your sentiments about eating originate from and restructure them to meet your reality.

As another example, say you grew up playing competitive sports and were pushed by your parents to be the greatest on the team. As an adult, you can struggle with remaining active for your health, instead feeling an internal pressure to be excellent at everything and satisfy people around you. By reconnecting with your inner child, you may learn to embrace exercise for what it is now: not as a display of power or talent, but as a kind of self-care that you can genuinely enjoy.

As a result, inner child work may help you enjoy yourself more and shed the fears you've brought into adulthood. It helps you understand yourself better, and it makes it simpler to pursue your pleasure and passion in daily life.

22 WAYS TO CONNECT WITH YOUR INNER CHILD
1. GET MESSY.
Give yourself permission to create a mess doing something you love—be that baking, painting, applying your makeup, playing with play-doh, whatever. Sure, you'll have to clean it up later, but it'll be worth the joy and freedom of creating a mess for once.

2. TREAT YOURSELF TO SOMETHING RIDICULOUS.
Like an ice cream cone the size of your head or a lovely toy animal that attracts your attention. There's no shame in treating yourself to and enjoying something "silly," and it'll restore that Christmas morning-type excitement from

childhood. Find a bouncy castle, arrange a fairy-themed party, climb a tree or sleep on the opposite side of the bed.

3. FOLLOW A BODY SCAN MEDITATION.

As you develop, you lose your fundamental connection with your body. Follow a body scan meditation on Spotify or Youtube to feel and explore your body.

4. SPEAK YOUR TRUTH.

Children don't have filters. While I don't advocate getting rid of yours totally, try being honest about how you feel. Start small by speaking out about the restaurant you prefer for supper or turning down a social request when you need rest.

5. TAKE A NATURE WALK.

Not a strenuous trek with a goal, but a pure nature stroll. Pick a nearby park or path, and take your time exploring your surroundings. Stop to gaze at flowers, absorb the vistas, or listen to birds.

6. WRITE YOURSELF A LETTER.

Write a letter to your younger self. Think about what she needed to hear back then. Send her words of encouragement, soothe her, and share with her what your life is like today.

7. SPEND TIME WITH KIDS.

Nothing can reunite you with your inner child quite like spending a few hours playing make-believe with your nieces and nephews or your friends' youngsters. Next time someone needs a babysitter, offer!

8. RE-READ A BOOK FROM YOUR CHILDHOOD.

Pick yourself a copy of Junie B. Jones or Ramona and Beezus from your local library, and reward yourself with an easy read. Trust me, as soon as you start reading, the memories of the first time you read it will come rushing back to you.

9. DO SOMETHING PURPOSEFULLY DESTRUCTIVE.

When was the last time you broke anything on purpose? Shred paper, hurl ice cubes at the pavement, punch a pillow if you have to! As adults, we learn to suppress fury and dissatisfaction. Let it out in a physical manner!

10. SPEAK TO YOUR INNER CHILD.

The next time you find yourself feeling terrified or anxious, speak to your inner child. Tell her she'll be all right, and talk sweetly to her. You'd be shocked how much speaking aloud to yourself can ease your worries.

11. TRY ARTS AND CRAFTS.

Let yourself be creative without the pressure to be flawless. Buy a coloring book, construct a friendship bracelet, or paint a birdhouse. It doesn't have to come out flawless (or even decent, for that matter) (or even good, for that matter). Just enjoy the process!

12. PLAN A SLEEPOVER.

Forget meeting over coffee. Plan a sleepover with your closest buddies! Stay up late munching, making a pillow fort, watching movies, and conversing. You'll get to reconnect with your inner adolescent, and you'll get even closer to your buddies (who, believe me, will have fun) (who, trust me, will have a blast).

13. PRACTICE MEDITATION AND MINDFULNESS.

Mindfulness activities let us get into our subconscious thoughts and emotions. While you're practicing, try to look back to your greatest childhood memories and pinpoint instances in your current life when those same sentiments come up. Or, if you're not into guided meditations, try a sunbathing practice.

14. DANCE AROUND THE HOUSE.

Put on your favorite song and dance like no one's watching (since technically, no one is)! It's a terrific way to feel in tune with your body and release anxious energy. Plus, it's just simple fun!

15. MAKE YOURSELF LAUGH.

When you're feeling uptight, throw on your favorite amusing movie or watch that Youtube video that never fails to make you laugh. Just as we learn to restrain wrath, we also learn to tone down our delight. Permit yourself to laugh.

16. JOURNAL ABOUT LIFE, PAST AND PRESENT.

While you're writing, remember back to your greatest childhood recollections. Where were you, who were you with, and what did you feel? As you dive deep into these recollections, you can unearth feelings you didn't know you were experiencing at the time.

17. VOLUNTEER.

How frequently do you perform something that 1) doesn't instantly benefit you and 2) you aren't being compensated for? Choose a local charity and volunteer a few days a month. Chances are, it'll be the first time in a while you've worked for anything simply for the fun of it.

18. LOOK AT YOUR BABY PHOTOS.

Ask your parents for your baby photographs and old yearbooks. Spend time reminiscing about your past lessons, interests, and yes, even your wardrobe choices. Seeing how youthful you seem in these images could offer you a fresh perspective on who you were back then.

19. REKINDLE A CHILDHOOD PASSION.

Did you spend all your childhood weekends watching backyard bugs, hula hooping, or practicing piano? Why not revive that youthful enthusiasm as an adult? Pick up an old passion, and connect with your inner kid through a common interest.

20. SET ASIDE TIME FOR DAYDREAMING AND VISUALIZATION.

Thanks to our phones and laptops, we've grown unaccustomed to boredom. Experience purposeful boredom by sitting in a quiet spot and letting your thoughts wander. If you don't feel like you have time for daydreaming, try establishing more time freedom in your life.

21. MAKE YOUR FAVORITE MEAL FROM CHILDHOOD.

Remember your favorite dish from childhood, the one you always got thrilled about? Treat yourself to it like an adult! Make it at home while listening to your favorite music, or take yourself on a single dinner date.

22. RECONNECT WITH AN OLD FRIEND.

Reach out to a childhood buddy you haven't talked to in a while. Ask how they're doing, ask about their family, and let them know you're thinking about them. Who knows? You may maybe revive an old relationship.

WANT TO MAKE MORE TIME FOR THE THINGS YOU LOVE?

Reconnecting with your inner child is a terrific approach to alleviate some of the stress of adult life.

There is a kid in everyone. But occasionally, people forget to embrace the humorous, lighter side of life. Reconnecting with your inner kid involves taking life a bit less seriously. It is giving oneself time to play, explore, laugh, and observe the world with both delight and amazement.

Play!

Adult duties, like paying the bills or doing errands, might make you take life too seriously occasionally. Everyone has to get out of their shell every once and a while. Dance with buddies. Run about in a field. Have a water balloon battle. Have a nice chuckle. When you approach life with a playful mentality, ordinary occurrences become fascinating, amusing, and enjoyable!

Even when you deal with challenging circumstances, such as in the office or during social encounters, you may employ fun to ease stress. This free-spirited, joyful personality provides you with a more optimistic view so you can deal with life in constructive, healthy ways.

Research published in Frontiers of Psychology analyzes how adult playfulness provides a full array of advantages, such as enhanced job and academic performance and greater creativity and drive. People who stay fun and youthful at heart live longer!

Express yourself truthfully and honestly
Children appear to boldly express themselves by dancing, laughing, and playing! They surely

know how to tell it like it is, too, and sometimes they are brutally honest!

As you get older, cultural conventions tend to impact your habits. You may feel timid or frightened to express yourself. You may speak up less, possibly out of fear of rejection.

Your genuine self deserves to shine! When you hold back on expressing your actual sentiments, you lose out on crucial relationships and experiences. Channel your inner kid again by learning to speak freely and honestly. Not everyone may enjoy what you have to say, and that's alright! When you express yourself, you provide your unique viewpoint to the world and eventually attract individuals who appreciate you.

Spend time with children
What better way to bring out your inner child than to spend more time with kids? Whether you are cracking jokes, running around, or playing games, finding time to spend with your

kids helps tap into your inner fun and youthful expression. You also get to contribute your expertise to assist young ones to learn and flourish. If you don't have children, you could spend time with the children of your friends or family.

Embrace learning
Adults prefer to concentrate on problem-solving and getting things done. Children live with an openness to learn and experience the world with all of its possibilities. You may connect to your inner child by letting go of the impulse to correct and control all the time. Instead, have an open mind and observe the learning possibilities around you each day.

Look up!
Sometimes individuals perceive life in tunnel vision, glancing down at their phone displays or racing to the next appointment. Take a time to stop and gaze up into the sky. The light, the clouds, the moon, and the stars will remind you

to halt once in a while, to enjoy your environment like a kid.

Get creative
Kids love to learn via arts and crafts, dance, drawing, singing, you name it! You can bring out your inner kid, too, via creative activity—and gain tons of added health advantages.

According to Medical News Today, creative self-expression helps deal with trauma, control emotions, and increases overall wellness.

Need some inspiration? You can discover lots of adult coloring books to get your creative juices flowing. Or, start some DIY projects for adorning your house or business.

Heal the wounded inner child
Much of your personality and habits form throughout the early stages of life. As you become older, you may continue to act out

patterns learned from infancy without recognizing them.

When you find yourself trapped in life, you may need to repair the wounded inner child. According to The American Journal of Psychotherapy, cognitive behavioral therapists typically have patients reconnect to the inner child to cure themselves of maladaptive emotional and behavioral patterns developed while growing up. In order release negative cycles, it involves mending the wounds of the past.

Close your eyes. Imagine yourself as a tiny kid again. What would you say to the youngster to console them? You may even compose a letter to assist your inner kid. This exercise will help heal wounds from the past and cultivate self-compassion. You'll have an easier time forgiving yourself for errors you hang onto when you picture yourself as an innocent kid.

True maturity is to nurture and listen to that inner kid. It means to listen to the wounds of the past, react to their needs, and heal. When you reconnect with your inner child, you become more aware of the motives underlying your actions, emotions, and relationships. Through that process of inner awareness.

Chapter 2

Emotional and psychological trauma and PTSD.

Emotional and Psychological Trauma
When bad things happen, it can take a while to get over the pain and feel safe again. But with these self-help strategies and support, you can speed up your recovery.
Young woman on the sofa, arms clasped around knees, hand covering mouth, anxious

What is emotional and psychological trauma?
Emotional and psychological trauma is the result of extraordinarily stressful events that shatter your sense of security, making you feel helpless in a dangerous world. Psychological trauma can leave you struggling with upsetting emotions, memories, and anxiety that won't go away. It can also leave you feeling numb, disconnected, and unable to trust other people.

Traumatic situations frequently include danger to life or safety, but any circumstance that leaves you feeling overwhelmed and alienated may end in trauma, even if it doesn't involve physical injury. It's not the factual conditions that decide whether an incident is traumatic, but your subjective emotional experience of the event. The more afraid and powerless you feel, the more likely you are to be traumatized.

Emotional and psychological trauma may be induced by:

One-time incidents, such as an accident, injury, or a violent assault, particularly if it was unexpected or occurred in infancy.

Ongoing, unrelenting stress, such as living in a crime-ridden area, suffering a life-threatening disease, or enduring traumatic experiences that recur frequently, such as bullying, marital abuse, or childhood mistreatment.

Commonly neglected reasons, such as surgery (particularly in the first 3 years of life), the abrupt loss of someone close, the dissolution of an important relationship, or a humiliating or severely disappointing event, especially if someone was purposefully harsh.

Coping with the trauma of a natural or manufactured catastrophe may provide unique challenges—even if you weren't personally engaged in the event. In reality, although it's exceedingly unlikely any of us will ever be the direct victims of a terrorist attack, aircraft accident, or mass shooting, for example, we're all routinely assaulted with awful photos on social media and news sources of those individuals who have been. Viewing these sights again and over might overload your nervous system and induce severe stress. Whatever the origin of your trauma, and whether it occurred years ago or yesterday, you may make therapeutic adjustments and go on with your life.

Childhood trauma and the risk of future trauma

While traumatic events may happen to anybody, you're more likely to be traumatized by an incident if you're already under a significant stress load, have recently experienced a series of losses, or have been traumatized before—especially if the previous trauma happened in infancy. Childhood trauma may occur from anything that interrupts a child's feeling of safety, including:

An unstable or unsafe environment
Separation from a parent
Serious illness
Intrusive medical procedures
Sexual, physical, or verbal abuse
Domestic violence
Neglect
Experiencing trauma in childhood might result in a severe and long-lasting impact. When childhood trauma is not addressed, a feeling of dread and powerlessness continues over into adulthood, creating the scene for subsequent trauma. However, even if your trauma happened many years ago, there are steps you can take to overcome the pain, learn to trust and connect to others again, and regain your sense of emotional balance.

Symptoms of psychological trauma
We all react to trauma in different ways, experiencing a wide range of physical and emotional reactions. There is no "right" or "wrong" way to think, feel, or respond, so don't

judge your reactions or those of other people. Your responses are NORMAL reactions to ABNORMAL events.

Emotional & psychological symptoms:

Shock, denial, or disbelief
Confusion, difficulty concentrating
Anger, irritability, mood swings
Anxiety and fear
Guilt, shame, self-blame
Withdrawing from others
Feeling sad or hopeless
Feeling disconnected or numb
Physical symptoms:

Insomnia or nightmares
Fatigue
Being startled easily
Difficulty concentrating
Racing heartbeat
Edginess and agitation
Aches and pains
Muscle tension
Healing from trauma

Trauma symptoms typically last from a few days to a few months, gradually fading as you process the unsettling event. But even when you're feeling better, you may be troubled from time to time by painful memories or emotions—especially in response to triggers such as an anniversary of the event or something that reminds you of the trauma.

If your psychological trauma symptoms don't ease up—or if they become even worse—and you find that you're unable to move on from the event for a prolonged period, you may be experiencing Post-Traumatic Stress Disorder (PTSD). While emotional trauma is a normal response to a disturbing event, it becomes PTSD when your nervous system gets "stuck" and you remain in psychological shock, unable to make sense of what happened or process your emotions.

Whether or not a traumatic event involves death, you as a survivor must cope with the loss, at least temporarily, of your sense of safety. The natural reaction to this loss is grief. Like people who have lost a loved one, you need to go through a grieving process. The following tips can help you cope with the sense of grief, heal from the trauma, and move on with your life.

Trauma recovery tip 1: Get moving
Trauma disrupts your body's natural equilibrium, freezing you in a state of hyperarousal and fear. As well as burning off adrenaline and releasing endorphins, exercise and movement can help repair your nervous system.

Try to exercise for 30 minutes or more on most days. Or if it's easier, three 10-minute spurts of exercise per day are just as good.

Exercise that is rhythmic and engages both your arms and legs—such as walking, running, swimming, basketball, or even dancing—works best.

Add a mindfulness element. Instead of focusing on your thoughts or distracting yourself while you exercise, really focus on your body and how it feels as you move. Notice the sensation of your feet hitting the ground, for example, the rhythm of your breathing, or the feeling of wind on your skin. Rock climbing, boxing, weight training, or martial arts can make this easier—after all, you need to focus on your body movements during these activities to avoid injury.

You don't have to talk about the trauma. Connecting with others doesn't have to involve talking about the trauma. In fact, for some people, that can just make things worse. Comfort comes from feeling engaged and accepted by others.

Ask for support. While you don't have to speak about the trauma itself, you must have someone to discuss your experiences with face to face, someone who will listen carefully without judging you. Turn to a trustworthy family member, friend, counselor, or pastor.

Participate in social events, even if you don't feel like it. Do "normal" activities with other people, activities that have nothing to do with the traumatic incident.

Reconnect with old pals. If you've withdrawn from connections that were previously essential to you, make the effort to reconnect.

Join a support group for trauma sufferers. Connecting with people who are suffering the same challenges may help minimize your feeling of isolation, and hearing how others deal can help encourage you in your recovery.

Volunteer. As well as helping others, volunteering may be a terrific way to fight the feeling of powerlessness that frequently follows trauma. Remind yourself of your abilities and restore your feeling of power by helping others.

Make new pals. If you live alone or distant from family and friends, it's crucial to seek out and create new connections. Take a class or join a club to meet others with similar interests, connect to an alumni organization, or reach out to neighbors or work colleagues.

If connecting to people is difficult...

Many individuals who have suffered trauma feel alienated, and withdrawn and find it difficult to connect with other people. If that describes you, there are certain activities you may do before you next meet with a friend:

Exercise or motion. Jump up and down, swing your arms and legs, or simply flail about. Your head will feel clearer and you'll find it easier to connect.

Vocal toning. As strange as it sounds, vocal toning is a great way to open up to the social engagement. Sit up straight and simply make "mmmm" sounds. Change the pitch and volume until you experience a pleasant vibration in your face.

Tip 3: Self-regulate your nervous system
No matter how agitated, anxious, or out of control you feel, it's important to know that you can change your arousal system and calm yourself. Not only will it help relieve the anxiety associated with trauma, but it will also engender a greater sense of control.

Mindful breathing. If you are feeling bewildered, confused, or agitated, practicing mindful breathing is a simple approach to calm yourself. Simply take 60 breaths, concentrating your attention on each 'out-breath.

Sensory input. Does a certain sight, scent, or flavor rapidly make you feel calm? Or maybe caressing an animal or listening to music serves to fast settle you? Everyone reacts to sensory input a little differently, so try various rapid stress reduction tactics to discover what works best for you.

Staying grounded. To feel in the present and more grounded, sit on a chair. Feel your feet on the ground and your back against the chair. Look around you and identify six items that have red or blue in them. Notice how your breathing grows deeper and calmer.

Allow yourself to experience what you feel when you feel it. Acknowledge your emotions regarding the trauma as they come and accept them. HelpGuide's Emotional Intelligence Toolkit may assist.

Tip 4: Take care of your health

It's true: having a healthy physique may boost your capacity to deal with the stress of trauma.

Get lots of sleep. After a stressful encounter, anxiety or dread may alter your sleep habits. But a lack of quality sleep might increase your trauma symptoms and make it difficult to maintain your emotional equilibrium. Go to sleep and get up at the same time each day and strive for 7 to 9 hours of sleep each night.

Avoid drinking and drugs. Their usage may intensify your trauma symptoms and cause feelings of melancholy, anxiety, and isolation.

Eat a well-balanced diet. Eating modest, well-balanced meals throughout the day can help you keep your energy up and reduce mood fluctuations. Avoid sugary and fried meals and consume enough omega-3 fats—such as salmon, walnuts, soybeans, and flaxseeds—to give your mood a boost.

Reduce stress. Try relaxing methods such as meditation, yoga, or deep breathing exercises. Schedule time for things that offer you delight such as your favorite hobbies.

When to seek professional counseling for trauma
Recovering from trauma takes time, and everyone recovers at their rate. But if months have passed and your symptoms aren't easing up, you may need professional therapy from a trauma specialist.

Seek therapy for trauma if you're:

Having problems functioning at home or work
Suffering from acute dread, anxiety, or sadness
Unable to develop intimate, rewarding connections
Experiencing horrific recollections, nightmares, or flashbacks
Avoiding more and more everything that reminds you of the trauma
Emotionally numb and distant from others
Using drinks or drugs to feel better

Working through trauma may be dangerous, difficult, and sometimes re-traumatizing, therefore this healing process is best completed with the guidance of an experienced trauma expert. Finding the proper therapist may take some time. The therapist you pick must have expertise in treating trauma. But the quality of the interaction with your therapist is as crucial. Choose a trauma expert you are comfortable with. If you don't feel comfortable, respected, or understood, find another therapist.

Ask yourself:

Did you feel comfortable expressing your difficulties with the therapist?
Did you feel like the therapist understood what you were talking about?
Were your concerns handled seriously or were they downplayed or dismissed?
Were you handled with compassion and respect?
Do you suppose that you could develop trust in the therapist?
Treatment for trauma

To recover from psychological and emotional trauma, you'll need to resolve the unpleasant sensations and memories you've long avoided, release pent-up "fight-or-flight" energy, learn to manage powerful emotions, and regain your capacity to trust other people. A trauma expert may employ a range of different therapeutic techniques in your treatment.

The somatic experience focuses on body sensations, rather than ideas and recollections regarding the traumatic incident. By focusing on what's occurring in your body, you may release pent-up trauma-related energy via shaking, weeping, and other types of physical release.

Cognitive-behavioral therapy helps you analyze and assess your ideas and emotions regarding a trauma.

EMDR (Eye Movement Desensitization and Reprocessing) mixes components of cognitive-behavioral therapy with eye movements or other types of rhythmic, left-right stimulation that help "unfreeze" painful memories.

Helping a loved one cope with trauma
When a loved one has undergone trauma, your support may play a significant part in their rehabilitation.

Be patient and understanding. Healing from trauma takes time. Be patient with the rate of rehabilitation and realize that everyone's reaction to trauma is different. Don't evaluate your loved one's reaction against your response or anybody else's.

Offer practical assistance to help your loved one get back into a routine. That may involve assisting with getting groceries or doing cleaning, for example, or just being ready to speak or listen.

Don't rush your loved one into talking but be accessible if they want to chat. Some trauma survivors find it difficult to speak about what occurred. Don't push your loved one to open up but let them know you are there to listen if they want to chat, or available to simply hang out if they don't.

Help your loved one to mingle and unwind. Encourage them to participate in physical exercise, seek out friends, and pursue hobbies and other activities that please them. Take a fitness class together or set a regular lunch date with friends.

Don't take the trauma symptoms personally. Your loved one may become angry, irritable, withdrawn, or emotionally distant. Remember that this is a product of the trauma and may not have anything to do with you or your relationship.

To assist a youngster heal from trauma, it's crucial to talk honestly. Let them know that it's natural to feel terrified or unhappy. Your kid may also look to you for indications on how they should react to trauma, so let them witness you healthily coping with your symptoms.

How children respond to emotional and psychological stress

Some frequent responses to trauma and techniques to help your kid cope with them:

Regression. Many youngsters need to return to an earlier period when they felt safer. Younger children may wet the bed or desire a bottle; older children may dread being alone. It's crucial to be empathetic, patient, and reassuring if your kid reacts this way.

Thinking the incident is their fault. Children younger than 8 tend to assume that if anything goes wrong, it must be their fault. Be sure your youngster knows that he or she did not cause the tragedy.

Sleep problems. Some youngsters have difficulties falling asleep; others wake often or have unpleasant nightmares. Give your youngster a plush animal, warm blanket, or flashlight to take to bed. Try spending additional time together in the evening, enjoying calm hobbies like reading. Be patient. It may take a long before your kid can sleep through the night again.

Feeling helpless. Being active in a campaign to prevent an event from happening again, writing thank you letters to people who have helped, and caring for others can bring a sense of hope and control to everyone in the family.

Chapter 3

Phases of the healing process

Reclaiming and Championing Your Inner Child, the process of mending your injured inner child is one of grieving, and it entails these six stages.

1. Trust

For your wounded inner child to come out of hiding, he must be able to trust that you will be there for him. Your inner child also needs a caring, non-shaming ally to affirm his abandonment, neglect, abuse, and enmeshment. Those are the initial crucial aspects of original pain work.

2. Validation

If you're still tempted to downplay and/or excuse how you were chastised, neglected, or used to nourish your parents, you need now to face the reality that these acts harmed your soul. Your parents weren't terrible, they have just wounded kids themselves.

3. Shock & Anger

If this is all startling to you, that's excellent, since the shock is the beginning of mourning.

It's normal to feel upset, even if what was done to you was inadvertent. You have to feel furious if you want to heal your wounded inner child. I don't mean you need to yell and holler (although you may) (although you might). It's simply acceptable to be upset about a shady transaction.

I know [my parents] did the best that two wounded adult children could do. But I'm also aware that I was wounded spiritually and that it's had life-damaging effects on me. What it means is that I hold us all accountable to stop what we're doing to ourselves and others. I will not accept the blatant dysfunction and abuse that ruled my family system.

4. Sadness

After rage comes to pain and grief. If we were victimized, we must lament that betrayal. We must also lament what might've been–our goals and aspirations. We must lament our unmet developmental requirements.

5. Remorse

When we mourn for someone who's gone, guilt is sometimes more important; for instance, maybe we wish we'd spent more time with the departed individual. But in mourning childhood abandonment, you must let your wounded inner child recognize that there was nothing he could've done differently. His anguish is about what happened to him; it's about him

6. Loneliness

The most basic sentiments of grieving are poisonous shame and loneliness. We were disgraced by [our parents] leaving us. We believe we are awful as if we're polluted, and that humiliation leads to loneliness. Since our inner kid feels imperfect and defective, he needs to cover up his actual self with his adapted, counterfeit self. He then learns to identify himself with his phony persona. His actual self stays alone and alienated.

Staying with this final layer of unpleasant sensations is the toughest aspect of the bereavement journey. "The only way out is through," we say in therapy. It's hard to remain at that level of guilt and loneliness; however, when we accept these sensations, we emerge out the other side. We confront the self that's been in hiding. You see, since we concealed it from others, we hid it from ourselves. In accepting our humiliation and loneliness, we begin to touch our genuine selves.

Signs of trust problems
Causes of lack of trust
How to overcome trust concerns
Recap

What some individuals label "trust issues" may be thoughts and actions tied to your attachment type and prior experiences. If unaddressed, they may damage every relationship in your life.

"Trust issues" is a word tossed about carelessly, frequently to describe when someone demonstrates chronic habits of mistrust, especially in personal relationships. It encourages the stigmatization of difficult emotional issues.

Chronic mistrust may damage how you perceive yourself and all the relationships in your life. You could find you constantly mistrust other people will follow through on their responsibilities, for example, or you may be frightened of getting too close to others or feel suspicious when someone is good to you.

Some of the behaviors linked with a problem trusting people might make partnerships tough, but they don't always have to do with the relationship itself.

What are the indications of 'trust issues?

What some label "trust issues" may be concerned with intimacy and bonding that might show as:

persistent jealousy
self-doubt
persistent suspicion
ongoing phony accusations
signs of anxiousness
avoidant habits
needy behaviors

emotional sensitivity or reactivity
unwillingness or inability to forgive
abandonment fear
indicators of codependency
Paranoia vs. trust concerns
Distrust is not the same as paranoia. Distrust often has roots in reality – you've encountered something that's made you distrust the dependability of others.

Paranoia is described as illogical, excessive distrust and mistrust.

"Where trust is founded on learned experiences, paranoia has no genesis story. With paranoia, there isn't evidence to justify the mistrust thrown on a person or experience," says Kali Wolken, a professional mental health counselor in Grand Rapids, Michigan.

Paranoia is commonly related to delusional illnesses, situations where you firmly believe in something incorrect.

Where does lack of trust originate from?

Several ideas on the framework of trust and mistrust exist, but in 2005, researchers studied the strong link between trust and the demand for control.

They discovered that when you don't experience a feeling of control, you're less likely to generate favorable expectations of others, a critical element of trust.

Why you may not feel in control may depend on your prior experiences and present circumstances.

Possible reasons include:

trauma
unloving childhood
rejection in childhood
past relationship experiences
insecure attachment style
mental health problems
Trauma
Living with certain side effects of trauma, particularly long-term, persistent levels of mistrust, is normal.

Trauma may be so significant that a study from 2020 states that mental health practitioners must build a foundation for trust between them and persons living with trauma, so those people can go and develop trust in their other relationships.

Hurtful childhood
Maltreatment throughout childhood doesn't have to be a unique, catastrophic event. It might be exposed to long-term or dangerous practices that become destructive over time.

A 2021 study by a trusted Source on childhood abuse revealed, like trauma, it was closely associated with levels of mistrust. The more extreme childhood maltreatment was, the more resistant distrust was to change with positive feedback.

Past relationship experiences
Known as "betrayal trauma" or "trauma committed by close others," these incidents trigger a shattering of trust in a relationship.

For many individuals, this is an act of adultery. Still, it may also be an encounter so unexpected that breaks a strong connection with family or friends, such as acts of theft or sabotage.

In 2014, researchers discovered, consistent with earlier studies, that those with betrayal trauma experiences were less trusting of romantic relationships and others in general. However, ordinary trusting habits generally did not seem much changed.

Attachment style
Attachment style theory states that how you connect with your main caregivers as a kid strongly affects how you create relationships as an adult.

Insecure attachment patterns are regarded to be the outcome of parents who didn't satisfy specific requirements when they were growing up.

For example, uneven parenting may have led to an anxious attachment style, commonly related to abandonment dread later in life.

In 2015, a study by trusted Sources examining mistrust in romantic relationships revealed that attachment style was closely associated with the amount of distrust in a relationship. Distrust predicted behaviors including envy, nonphysical aggression, psychological abuse, and nosy actions.

Mental health diseases
Certain mental health conditions may feature signs of mistrust or paranoia, including:

post-traumatic stress disorder (PTSD)
paranoid personality disorder
dependent personality disorder
psychosis/psychotic disorders
depressed disorders
anxiety disorders
Natural mistrust
It's common to have some amount of distrust, or overall anxiety, even regularly.

Everyday trust, the type of trust that enables you to stroll close to people on the street, is defined by:

familiarity
your innate tendency toward trust offered by your nature
trust in the information or expertise
Entering a foreign city with unfamiliar people, for example, might lead you to develop distrust.

How to overcome trust difficulties
Chronic mistrust may be a tough tendency to change, but it's not impossible to overcome.

Communicating
"When it comes to creating trust, honest and effective communication is essential," says Dr. Kamran Eshtehardi, a clinical psychologist in Pasadena, California.

Eshtehardi advocates expressing your difficulties with trust, letting people know your ideals, and stating where your boundaries are set.

Wolken advocates avoiding "you did this to me" during these dialogues and instead on "I felt this way," remarks.

An example might be: "I felt dissatisfied when you didn't come there on time." This grants ownership to your emotions rather than merely blaming the other person.

Wolken argues trust is more readily created when you're an active participant in the process. Communicating trust is the first step.

Allowing individuals the ability to alter
If your skepticism arises from someone's behaviors, Wolken thinks the best approach to regain trust is to provide that person an opportunity to prove themselves.

To achieve this, honest discussion about the situation is a requirement, and clear expectations have to be made.

Example: "I feel upset when you're late to key occasions. On Saturday, I'd love it if you were there on time."

If behaviors that erode trust persist despite open discussion, it may be time to reassess that partnership.

Finding a location for trustworthy individuals
When someone hasn't given you any cause to distrust them, Kevin Coleman, a marital and family therapist in Columbia, South Carolina, proposes establishing an emotional starting place for them.

"Identify one tiny area where you could allow them in emotionally speaking, and one small step at a time, you can trust them a bit more than you used to," he adds.

This might entail opening up to them about your favorite pastime, for example, or telling them something significant about your family.

Validating what you're experiencing
Coleman also advocates evaluating your sentiments when you're experiencing suspicion.

By outlining why you mistrust someone, you may take a step back from mistaken beliefs and ask yourself whether they have a factual foundation.

Writing your thoughts in a notebook may help you explain what you're feeling and can help you find patterns in persistent mistrust toward several persons.

Professional advice
The foundations of persistent mistrust typically come from key life events. In addition to trust issues, you may live with other challenges, including mental health disorders.

Speaking with a mental health expert may assist.

You may work together toward analyzing the origins and implications of the initial incident that produced persistent mistrust. A mental health expert may also help you explore new avenues for creating and sustaining trust.

Let's recap

If you've been told you have "trust issues," folks may be referring to patterns of mistrust they notice reoccur across your relationships. In reality, you don't "have issues" but rather probably live with the psychological effects of a significant life experience.

Chronic distrust can come from a traumatic incident, an unloving childhood, or experienced betrayal in other relationships.

Overcoming trust challenges often involves understanding where these feelings come from. A mental health expert may assist and guide you in the process of healing.

Today, self-care is more commonly addressed than ever before- and for good reason. Healthcare experts and therapists alike are offering strategies to decrease calm, relieve anxiety, and make the current moment as tranquil as possible.

Yet, what do you do when your anxieties, trauma, and pain extend much deeper than the present events you're experiencing? How do you commence healing when it's your inner child that's calling out for love, acceptance, and comfort?

Learning how to confront the past without allowing it to dictate your present and future might be a tough step to take, but it is achievable. Today, we're discussing seven methods you may tackle the problem that losing your innocence and start rebuilding the life you deserve.

1. Acknowledge Your Inner Child

Before you can start along the road of repair, you must admit that your inner child exists. Though it can seem ridiculous at first, speak to him or her if they were right by you.

Giving this individual a true identity will help him move through the challenges you encountered together. Start by uttering expressions of affirmation such as "I love you" and "I see you" in the mirror, or even envision saying this to your younger, wounded self.

You may find it simpler to explain these sentiments to your prior self via writing. If this is the case, compose letters to your inner kid that cover the same feelings. The idea is to provide the youngster with the sentiments of validation and affirmation that were lacking for so long.

2. Validate What Happened

Pushing them down or pushing them under the rug can only work for so long. If you've endured abuse, neglect, or any sort of trauma as a kid, it's vital to be realistic about what occurred.

With your inner child with you, take the time to grasp what occurred completely. This can involve going through the events in detail, or it might mean revisiting a persistent sense of shame or guilt. While such, it's ideal to finish this phase with a professional expert who can give coping skills as you take that unpleasant journey down memory lane.

3. Identify The Form Of Neglect You Experienced

Even children who grew up in an idyllic environment can have wounds that originated decades ago. After you've identified a specific area of hurt, consider the bigger picture surrounding that event or series of events.

At the core of much trauma lies some form of neglect. This might vary from a lack of affection to a lack of protection and everything in between. You could have wished you had more resources, more supervision, or more freedom. Allow yourself to experience that emptiness again, and identify it for what it is.

4. Embrace Your Emotions

Not every inner child's work will bring up emotions of bitterness or wrath, but some could. For instance, you may feel regret at your parents or upset at a friend or family member. Rather than attempting to get beyond those feelings, go ahead and sit with them.

This can entail suffering fury, despair, emptiness, or shame all over again. Talk to a therapist when these feelings go up to the surface. Often, the only way to get beyond them and achieve genuine healing is to address them head-first.

That said, be easy on yourself. You may not get through everything in one day or one visit, and that's OK. Give yourself room and time to comprehend the trip. Take pauses and seek help and direction from reliable friends, counselors, and coaches.

5. Identify Current Manifestations of Past Hurts

Do you find yourself participating in self-sabotaging practices that arise from prior childhood hurts? For instance, if you were abandoned when you were younger, you could now participate in toxic relationships with someone you know would forsake you down the line.

Or, you could project sentiments of skepticism and suspicion on individuals who truly want to be in your life, hesitant to allow them to get too close for fear that you'll finish up alone again.

Whatever the manner these old injuries present themselves now, it's crucial, to be honest with yourself and recognize them. Acknowledgment is the first step in moving ahead and making the adjustment toward better behaviors.

6. Take Steps to Fill the Gap

When you're younger, you fall prey to your circumstances because you are unable to stand against them. As an adult, you may take proactive actions to provide for yourself the things you wish you'd had as a kid.

For instance, if you were in a cycle of poverty in your youth, you can take steps to improve your current financial outlook. Partner with an expert who can teach you how to budget, save for the future, and maximize your income. Or, if you felt neglected and invisible as a child, seek relationships with people who cherish their time with you and make time to keep those friendships alive.

In other words, give yourself what you wish your parents or guardians would have given you years ago and allow yourself to enjoy the freedom that comes with that reward.

7. Mend the Hurt By Helping Others

Research shows that child abuse, neglect and mistreatment is a global issue, affecting millions of children each year. While you can't go back in time and change your past, there are plenty of ways you can help change the future for someone who's now in your shoes.

From volunteering at a children's home to serving meals at a homeless shelter, look for opportunities in your community where you can give back, especially if it means making a difference in the life of a young boy or girl. Even just lending a listening, empathetic ear to a friend or acquaintance in need can be your form of service.

Understand that at first, these kinds of interactions might be triggering for you if they remind you

Chapter 4

Let go of your past

Everyone has an inner kid.
You could regard this inner kid as a direct reflection of yourself in your early years, a patchwork collection of the developmental phases you've lived through, or a sign of young hopes and fun.

An awareness of your inner child might help you look back to lighter, carefree years, "Being in touch with the pleasures of childhood may be a good method of coping with tough times."

Not everyone equates childhood with playfulness and joy, however. If you suffered neglect, trauma, or other emotional distress, your inner child could look little, helpless, and in need of care. You may have buried this anguish deep to conceal it and protect yourself — both your current self and the kid you once were.

Hiding suffering doesn't cure it. Instead, it typically appears in your adult life, showing up as difficulties in personal relationships or problems satisfying your own needs. Working to repair your inner child may help you handle some of these challenges.

Healing your inner child might take time, but these eight recommendations are a solid beginning point.

First, recognize your inner child
To begin healing, you first have to accept your inner child's existence.

anybody can come in touch with their inner child – provided they're open to exploring this connection. If you feel hesitant or averse to the concept of addressing the past, you'll have a tougher difficulty starting the healing process.

If it seems a bit unusual or difficult to contemplate opening up to your kid self, try thinking about inner child work as a journey of self-discovery.

Briefly lay aside the presence of your inner child and only think about a few crucial childhood memories. While some were certainly favorable, others may have harmed or angered you. Perhaps you still carry the emotional trauma from those occurrences now.

The act of addressing your inner child merely requires identifying and embracing things that caused you to anguish in childhood. Bringing these wounds out into the light of day might help you begin to grasp their effect.

That said, many individuals do find it beneficial, even comforting, to treat their inner child as they would a live person, so don't feel hesitant to give it a try.

Listen to what your inner kid has to say
After opening the door to a connection with your inner child, it's crucial to listen to the emotions that come.

"These sensations typically come up in circumstances that elicit intense emotions, discomfort, or past wounds," Egel adds.

You may notice:

rage over unfulfilled needs
abandonment or rejection
insecurity
vulnerability
guilt or shame
anxiety
If you can trace these sentiments back to particular childhood experiences, you may recognize comparable circumstances in your adult life provoke the same reactions.

Here's an example:

Your spouse suddenly gets busy with work and doesn't have time for the big night out you'd planned. While you know they'd like to spend time with you, you nevertheless feel rejected and dissatisfied. Your dissatisfaction emerges in a juvenile fashion, with you storming off to your room and slamming the door.

Considering what transpired from the perspective of your inner child might give some helpful information in this case.

You realize your partner's unexpected need to work made you feel precisely like you felt when your parents canceled plans, playdates, or even your birthday party, due to their busy schedules.

In this manner, listening to the sensations of your inner child and allowing yourself to experience them instead of pushing them away may help you recognize and validate the discomfort you've experienced – a vital first step toward moving through it.

Write a letter
To create a discussion and start the healing process, Raab advocates drafting a letter to your inner child.

You may write about childhood recollections from your adult viewpoint, giving insight or answers for difficult conditions you didn't comprehend back then.

Maybe you didn't realize why your brother constantly yelled at you and damaged your toys, but you learned to dread him all the same. If you've now understood he underwent years of bullying and abuse, his wrath may begin to make sense. Sharing this understanding with your inner child will help heal some of that remaining anguish.

A letter might also provide you the opportunity to express words of encouragement and support.

A couple of questions might also help keep the debate going:

"How do you feel?

"

"How can I help you?
"

"What do you need from me?
"

Sitting with these questions may frequently lead to answers, however, it may take some time before your inner child feels comfortable and secure.

Give meditation a try

Those questions you asked your inner child? Meditation may be a terrific means of opening oneself up for answers.

Meditation offers numerous advantages for physical and mental health, but a handful of them link directly to inner child work.

For one, meditation promotes conscious self-awareness, training you to pay greater attention to emotions that come up in everyday life. Greater attention surrounding your emotions makes it simpler to identify when certain events generate harmful responses.

Meditation also helps you feel more comfortable with undesirable emotions.

Children sometimes have a hard time recognizing unpleasant feelings, particularly when they aren't encouraged to express themselves. They may ignore or bury these sensations to avoid punishment or obtain praise from caregivers for being "good" or keeping control.

Emotions, happy or bad, are designed to be experienced and expressed. Repressed emotions normally simply come up sometime down the road, frequently in unhelpful, even dangerous ways.

Meditation helps you practice noticing and sitting with any emotions that come up in your life. When you grow accustomed to embracing emotions as they occur, you'll find it easier to express them in healthy ways. This helps validate your inner child's sentiments by delivering the message that it's OK to experience emotions and let them out.

You may also attempt loving-kindness meditation to transmit sentiments of affection to your little self. Egel also offers visualization meditation as a good method for envisioning your inner child, or even "visiting" them as your adult self.

Journal as your inner kid

Many individuals find writing a useful tool to sift through tough or perplexing situations and emotional upheaval. If you maintain a diary, you could already derive a lot of benefits from this coping approach.

Just as writing may help you uncover patterns in your adult life that you wish to alter, journaling from the viewpoint of your inner child can help you recognize harmful patterns that originated in childhood.

For this writing practice, leave your current self aside for the moment and access your kid self. Try images or a quick visualization exercise to assist remember how you felt at the exact age you're aiming to investigate.

Once you're in the correct mentality, jot down a few memories and any feelings you connect with those occurrences. Try not to think too deeply about what you're writing. Just let the ideas flow onto the page as they come up. Expressing them in an unrestrained manner may help you reach the core of your inner child's suffering.

Bring back the pleasures of childhood
Adulthood undoubtedly comes with lots of obligations, but relaxation and fun are also crucial components of healthy mental health.

If your childhood lacked positive experiences, getting back in touch with your playful side and making time for fun can help heal the pain of missing out on what you needed as a child.

It's also crucial to appreciate simple joys, like ice cream after a walk, games with your spouse or children, and laughing with friends.

Whatever you do, making regular time for fun and lightheartedness in your life can help rekindle the positive emotions of youth.

Leave the door open
Healing doesn't always have a definite end. It's often more of an open-ended journey.

You've started the process by reaching out to your inner child. Now you can cultivate this newfound awareness and continue listening for your child self's guidance as you move forward.

Your child self may have more to reveal about challenges from the past. But you may also learn to become more spontaneous and fun and evaluate what life has to offer with a deeper sense of wonder.

Staying in touch with your inner child may lead to a more full sense of self and enhance confidence and drive. Reinforce the connection you've made by declaring your goal to continue listening, providing love and compassion, and trying to heal any wounds that remain open.

Talk to a therapist
Past trauma may bring a lot of discomforts. Therapists aim to establish a secure environment for you to begin navigating this emotional turbulence and discover useful skills for healing your inner child.

Therapists often realize how childhood traumas and other prior events may affect your life, relationships, and overall well-being. But not all styles of treatment promote the investigation of previous experiences or associated ideas, such as the inner child.

Cognitive behavioral therapy, for example, is regarded as a very successful therapeutic strategy, however, it often focuses on your experiences in the present.

If you're interested in undertaking some investigation of your history and getting to know your inner child, search for a therapist who has expertise in this area. Typically, psychodynamically focused psychotherapy might be a suitable match.

Inner child therapy, also called inner child work, specifically focuses on this process, but other types of therapists can also offer support. It always helps to let potential therapists know the specific concerns you'd like to explore.

The bottom line

When desires for affection, attention, praise, and other sorts of emotional support are unfulfilled in childhood, the trauma that occurs may linger far into your adult life.

But it's never too late to heal. By learning to nurture your inner child, you may affirm these needs, learn to express emotions in healthy ways, and promote self-compassion and self-love.

You've undoubtedly made a few allusions to your inner kid before.

"I'm channeling my inner child," you could claim, while leaping from swings at the park, chasing your roommate around the home with a Nerf pistol, or plunging into the pool with your clothes on.

Many credits the notion of an inner child to psychiatrist Carl Jung, who identified a child archetype in his writings. He related this internal child to previous experiences and recollections of innocence, fun, and inventiveness, along with optimism for the future.

your inner child as a manifestation of not only your kid self but your lived experience of all life phases. The inner child is also acknowledged as a source of strength, as early experiences may play a vital influence in your growth as an adult.

This may go both ways, though: When childhood events adversely impact you, your inner child may continue to bear these scars until you address the root.

"Each one of us has an inner child, or way of being, "Getting in touch with your inner child may assist develop well-being and offer a lightness to life."

Conclusion

Becoming your best self .

Why Our Inner Child Needs Attention

There is a component of our mind that keeps the feeling of inquiry, astonishment, and innocence we experienced as children. It keeps us asking questions about new things, playing and finding delight, and stimulates curiosity about the world around us. Our inner child, as it's known in psychology, may also hang onto the pain produced by feeling unsafe in our adolescence. This area of our mind could hang onto emotions of dread, anxiety, loneliness, or uncertainty we might have experienced as children, sentiments that subsequently find their way out into our thoughts, actions, and choices as adults. The impact of our inner child may wreak chaos in our life as it takes hold in difficult circumstances and drives our course depending on those sensations. We must learn to take up the responsibility of caring for our inner child's needs to recover and avoid allowing sorrow from our past to determine our present and future.

Understanding and Acknowledgement

Those who endured trauma and damage as children are not the only ones who could have felt unsafe while they were growing up. In reality, most individuals can certainly look back on pleasant childhoods attentively and discover situations where their needs were unsatisfied. There is no such thing as a perfect parent. It's the hardest duty anyone does, and in most situations, parents do the best they can with the knowledge, education, and maturity they have. Acknowledging where parents went short in making us feel secure isn't a process of seeking blame; it's merely for us to bring awareness to the emotions that lack of safety caused. There are many different ways that a child might feel unsafe; different types of abuse or neglect such as physical or emotional, lack of positive reinforcement, not being given the space for emotional expression, experiencing criticism or shame, or being pressured to achieve at a high level or grow up quickly is just a small list of examples.

To connect to one's inner child, there must be acceptance of these experiences and sentiments; basically, we must recognize not all of our needs were addressed and then take responsibility for caring for them ourselves as adults. We must become the parents that our inner kid needed and still needs and offer them a voice to communicate their sentiments to guarantee that we don't expect others and the environment around us to satisfy them.

A Relationship with Our Former Selves
How can one "re-parent" our inner child?

Open and sustain a conversation - One approach is to write a letter to and a letter from your inner child. An activity such as this may help open up the channels of communication between you and your inner child. This is one way many felt uncomfortable. As children, there wasn't an open discussion with our parents and we were left confused or misunderstood. Before we recognize our inner child, it's necessary to understand one of the reasons they "act out" through us, which is because they feel ignored.

If you need to, review your upbringing deeply to discover where this may have occurred, and to pinpoint areas your inner child felt unheard or frightened. Connect with them to ensure they are secure and to enable them to share their unpleasant emotions safely.

Nurture and love - Often our inner kid wants affection and comfort. Speaking this manner to ourselves, our inner child may assist alleviate bad sensations and provide the sense of protection they need. Guided meditations or visualizations frequently enhance this, enabling you to see yourself sitting next to yourself as a kid and allowing you the opportunity to embrace and hold them. You may also engage your inner kid by playing the way they want to, going to a park or amusement park, watching a movie you enjoyed as a child, coloring, or doing any other activity they'd enjoy.

Words of Affirmation - There are a variety of soothing and relaxing things that you may say to your inner child:

You are protected and cherished.

I support you/I will defend you.

It's alright to be sad/scared/anxious.

It's acceptable to say no.

I adore you the way you are.

You are kind/smart/funny/important.

I am delighted you are here.

Sharing - Talking with a trustworthy person, whether a therapist or a friend, is immensely essential to healing your inner child. Many of us have not had dialogues regarding the unpleasant situations we experienced as youngsters. Some of us may not even have realized that our experiences were unpleasant; talking about these things with a trustworthy person might help lessen the dread and anxiety surrounding them.

If we have not done the work to heal our inner child, we might struggle with trusting others, constant worry or anxiety, low self-esteem, or fear of new things, which can all lead to struggles navigating the world as adults. Becoming the parent we needed as children and recognizing the experiences we had may be tough and unpleasant; yet, it can help us develop life skills we may be missing, aid us with emotional control, build and enhance our relationships, and promote creativity and lightness.

Printed in Great Britain
by Amazon

18970087R00058